accidentally wild

by

Claudia Frick

Boulder, 2016

"come closer now, and listen
to love's restless rhythm
spreading like the tom-tom of African drums
through the hoah-hoah of my tribal limbs.
I ...sense it.
I....know the exact moment for prayer.
Now all the stars are making love!" - Forugh Farrokhzad

for my sweet sister Simone
whose hand I still feel in mine

for Mama
still miss you so

love love love

CONTENTS

on the fringe

munching on dandelion
suns, twirling tree
trunks, diving fences, hugging
walls   re-inventing
re-creating   cooking up love
unconditional

 late afternoon : a maddening knockkkk
 : I fall into the sorceress kitchen
the ceiling pressing down
on the silhouette of a bony creature :
Horch, wen die Nacht hereingeweht
: strange locks of gnarling brushwood
enfold my galloping heart   She gawks   she wonders

 I flee from truth hidden in dusty nooks; a copper cauldron
boiling over with answers to questions
                              wer o wer bin ich -
I don't dare to ask

hissing flames lick my mind   I erupt wildly
into a crack-in-the-pavement
prairie flower

my tongue can't form

this string of words   looping pipes
hold babble pockets like bird nests
in a gutter warped
by frozen rain

broken
sentences emerge
from hesitant   vibrations

Ich verliere deine Stimme, deinen Klang, deine
Schwingung. I choke

as I lose your timbre :   such longing
to live this fantastic world of dreams

unconstrained

where oceans are made of tears

hushed moan stuck
in my bones   I can't taste
sweet honey offered to me freely
by cottonwood trees & cumulous clouds   dying
stars & all the winged & crawling & leaping creatures

I heed the snap
crack of branches
not breaking into death, not grasping to each known fiber

It's more of a dismantling, a softening & melting
of molecules & cells
to rearrange

This the moment I surrender
O staune mein Herz das nicht zerbricht
 marveling at a heart
so brave

moon-embroidered

feathers spin me through air
tunnels. I chew on star petals
sink onto cloud beds steeped
in yearning : black weightless
whispers seep into time
loops : I am playing my part
in this theater of illusions
overstepping stones & truth
throwing off all shackles
to re-dream who I
am

ever wonder how still death is

shattering all you have known
your body opens, your senses
naked. The rose blossoms
until she bleeds black petals; each one
beautiful so
          beautiful.
A woodpecker unwavering
drums an untried beat awakening
the sleeping   afraid to die
into life

near-sleep experience

dreams haunt me: I count
my shame under thin linen   hushing
a heart's moan
to break loose from ropes I hold in my hands & wind so
tightly
around myself   inflicting
new wounds
burying me under the steamy
scent of sleeplessness   :   rollercoaster
battles spinning & twining
I stroke my belly
exhale deeply into my bones, into my shoulder blades
       desiring to fly as blackbird
electrifying flapping red wings

Don't doubt my sincere attempts to escape into sleep:
I applied hot & cold compresses. I drank hot passionflower
hops valerian chamomile tea. I oiled the sole of my feet in
magnesium. I meditated on moon light & invoked the dark
-robbed goddess Nyx.

stars trail down
my spine

invoked guest

the way you simmer a lamb stew
hour after hour and the way you desire
it to fall apart: so sweet so tender in your mouth.
The way your eyes are deep pools
in which ancient knowing is stored touching
bone deep to comprehend the untold. The way you pulse
alchemy, you pulse cumin coriander cinnamon & cayenne into lusciousness,
you feel my pulse:

it is too late to turn down
the fire: spluttering wildness you can't contain. Something
feral seeps through every pore.

You crave this

burning

a woman can't survive
after Joy Harjo

by her own breath
so I savor sweet raindrops
place my head onto melting ice
sway to the slow wild rhythm of wind
enfolding me in a cyclone of tales.
I reach towards the soft swish of maple leaves
hushing my rattling breath. White stripes of birch
wind around my body, milk oozes
over wounds and sometimes I taste
moist earth on my tongue
chew it unhurriedly with a snail's mind
snuggle into soft folds of earth & inhale
the coconut moon echoing
my prayers.

even if it burns

to be saved by beauty: this moment
the heavens on fire:
flickering stars, tingling sparks. A blossoming
accidentally wild   with purpose   without:
teasing out laughter on the lip of insanity
inciting earth pulse, swampy
blues pulse, the beat of pine mountain
grooves & late night blues pulse
nudging you loose-limbed, nuzzling
deep into your body

I soften into demons
that choke my truth, muffle my words, staple me
to constitutional pages   Today I sing, today
I rip out lying pages & throw out pain
killers tending to my soul call   moving as wind
flowing as water on this field where sharp edges yield
to gentleness   cuts mellow into smoothed
tear scars   where I invent new moves
imagine peace, believe
in love
just so

when the body rages

I shed my serpent skin bathing in moon light
and jaded bat song. Red yarn tangled
in my uterus: I summersault and cartwheel
spinning spinning until I forget. I surge
into free fall & fold & fall & break
open: remembering so little: soft words
about a poet dancing words. A dancer
who touches to heal. A healer who listens
to empower. To not overpower. To not undermine.
To not assume to know. To trust in a hand
of grace. To finally loose
myself

dancing spirit

after Maya Angelou's Phenomenal Woman

I am learning to see
my own beauty   gazing into the other
with a smile on my lips
with laugh lines around my eyes.
I start walking the way I dance
so every step is colorful:
the movements wide: I take up space
bear-like cat-   like

racing molecules

this: frosty glace
of the sun's heat: right here
more mellow, more like honey
seeping & revealing what's sacred
scared inside
of me.

How real dreams can become.
I feel the tide's pull
uprooting me. My shadow
offering herself to the light   a gift
        a graciousness

The way she blossoms, she dies

what is immortal

if it is not about getting to a certain place
if I am this   moment ushered
into being forgotten. If I let each tribulation each delight
have a voice. If I let the young girl covered under buttercup duvet
listening to every tint of silence and the notes in between
shuddering
under the bed she hid her nightmares
under the bed the nightmares hushed her
under the bed moon-milk trickled through mattress and board
              drowning her.
What if I allow space

I am a wave in this cosmic vastness. As you are.   I am
this droplet in the rain puddle. This whiff in the storm. As you are.
This stillness in the mountain lake. This singing. This weeping
into dry riverbeds.
As we all are
thirsty & drunk
so many desires shattered & showered by grace
If there is beauty
in each flower each bird each star blazing
as wild Prairie Fire

sweet love : what if

even the moon shuts her eyes
bewildered by this throbbing
ossifying of vows stitched in scarlet
smudges on a heart holy
& sinful

I carve a secret blood oath
& let the fire brew a biting nectar
of love : flowing, drooling from my mouth,
gashing tears. The long awaited flood. I slip over waves
swept under off my feet: I swallow ocean
tears. Flaming tremble of earth:
a love rhapsody!

Keep on   dancing
freely
down the road   oozing
love   locking eyes   hugging
bodies
everywhere

give me death

to feel one pea under one hundred soft mattresses
jolted   out of bed
my body   wide
awake: I heed the rustling
of layers shedding   a beckoning   to decipher
life's traces :
I'd taste Himalayan snow on the rim
of a singing bowl.   I'd brush against skin
that melts like chocolate in warm hemp milk.
I'd see crimson & scarlet, sapphire & cerulean, goldenrod & black
shaping infinite possibilities:
secrets held in adoration   dreams
slipping into space where night
& day   touch

touched in dance

in the dark cave of a new moon night
a candle cave, my womb on longing night's
moon, a wailing cup catching sacred moon
blood, a crimson petal cave
on a hidden moon night
luring me   kiss-drunk
into your body.
A new scent, an unknown taste on my tongue,
sliding thighs, slow moving
hips

I falter over this ragged night edge
feasting under honey
moon : making of new memory
moon : this moment
                untamed

blood-red petals

like this : I move my hips

slightly, the cushion pressing up:

I soften, I melt over-

flowing :

my lips still parched

my throat still yearns

       Every morning I get dressed & put on the serenity

mask : I juggle sounds. Lampposts lean

against an unfound rage. I balance on orbs   shooting pinballs

I nudge I trap I score

I charm the snake & wrap her tightly

around my throat to dam tear rivers

       Then I lose my mask (on purpose or not)

put her in a safety box (for who-knows-when)

bury her in the herb garden

       & resist her   for now

Like a volcano dormant for centuries

spewing & spitting

erupting   as never-ending

orgasms

        the earth cracks open, birthing

a new landscape

scarred but oh so beautiful

        leaving me

breathless

today I plant a moon rose

kleine Schwester worum weinst du

deine Traenen blutrot naehren diese Erde

und dir wachsen junge Wurzeln in dieser Umarmung

so zart mit Rot-Buche.

Du legst dich in ihre troestende Erdmulde

schmiegst dich

an deine verlorenTraeume heilig dieses schimmernde Licht

o, holy angel of death carry her gently

Dein Koerper so zart bricht aus in Flammen die dich verschlingen

Dein Herz stolpert ueber Knochen und Verlangen

tief in deinen Geliebten hinein.

O du, hast gerade zu tanzen begonnen

ungestuem und taumelnd

leaves fall in tear

drops

holy love prayer

1) May I not shy
away from love untamed tasting earth
colors & moonlight sheen in every kiss, adoring
valleys & mounds silken & knotted in you
in me. Old wounds & new ones held
and cared for so tenderly: this the sweet kind
of love the wild kind of love.

2) May I awaken : love-
crazed after being kissed this morning
touched this moment, roused by one sip
of wine. My beloved, you hold my undone heart
in your fire & I flow as water

3) As if we've touched each other
many life times before   as if I could draw from the spirit
world, as if I could be in time
with the musician & caress each string
shaping it into love
tones

4) May body & heart open as petals
necked by the sun. May we be still,
tending to each others scars. A love
where one can curl up in pain resting
until ready to unwrap & arms lift the other up
& we gaze into each other & commit fully
to this wild journey :
can you hear
how the earth gasps

Acknowledgments

Thank you, Lisa Birman, for your gentle guidance
and encouragement to make this poetry collection
the best it could be. Thanks to Jared Smith for
including 'on the fringe' & 'where oceans are made
of tears' into Turtle Island Quarterly Summer 2016.
I am grateful to the Innisfree poetry community
in Boulder that allowed me to dive deep and leap high.
Deep gratitude to everyone at the Community Holistic
Health Center in Lafayette who has embraced me
on this journey. I felt the love and cheering of so many
of my friends and family in the US and Austria.
You are the best.
Oh, Dominik, Daniel & Florian, I love you so much!
Henry, my dear husband, this haven I found in you!

Lightning Source UK Ltd.
Milton Keynes UK
UKRC012118280519
343495UK00006B/158